THE
HEALTHY
KITCHEN

VEGAN

hinkler

CONTENTS

Published by Hinkler Books Pty Ltd
45–55 Fairchild Street
Heatherton Victoria 3202 Australia
www.hinkler.com.au

Design © Hinkler Books Pty Ltd 2015
Food photography and recipe development
© Stockfood, The Food Media Agency
Typesetting: MPS Limited
Prepress: Graphic Print Group

ISBN: 978 1 7436 7734 6

Printed and bound in China

VEGAN

The Vegan Society was established in 1944, but evidence of people avoiding animal products dates back over two thousand years.

People choose veganism for health, environmental and moral reasons. Vegans abstain from foods of animal origin – fish, flesh and fowl – and also animal products and by-products, such as eggs, milk and gelatine. Some vegans may also choose not to wear clothing and shoes of animal origin, such as wool and silk. They may also abstain from using any products tested on animals. There are a few grey areas – some vegans will eat honey, for example.

Vegan diets generally are free from cholesterol, low in saturated fat and rich in fibre and nutrients. Vegans obtain their protein from legumes, such as beans, tofu and peanuts, and from grains, such as rice and corn. When following a vegan diet, you consume more fibre, so make sure you drink plenty of water.

This book contains a huge variety of recipes to help you plan healthy meals while following a vegan diet. Fruits, vegetables, nuts, grains, seeds, beans and legumes provide the basis of a variety of tasty dishes. Spinach, lentils and beans provide iron, while dried fruits, almonds and chickpeas (garbanzo beans) provide calcium.

When following any recipe, you can easily adapt it for a vegan diet by substituting vegan-friendly products. For example, you can substitute:

- soy yoghurt for yoghurt
- soy, almond or rice milk for milk
- maple syrup for honey
- agar agar for gelatine
- vegan cheese for cheese.

As the market for vegan foods grows, many vegan alternatives are now available for products such as cheese, milk, yoghurt and mayonnaise. Many supermarkets are beginning to stock more vegan-friendly ingredients; however, some items might be easier to find in health-food stores. In many areas, there are also vegan societies or networks that may be able to provide you with more information about following a vegan diet.

BREAKFAST

For a refreshing start to the day, choose a breakfast that doesn't come out of a box. These creative recipes use wholesome vegan ingredients that will help sustain your energy throughout the day.

STEWED APPLE BREAKFAST CUPS

Serves 4
Preparation and cooking 20 minutes

Ingredients:

500 g | 18 oz apples, cored, peeled and sliced
50 g | 1¾ oz | ¼ cup white (granulated) sugar, more if needed
1 tbsp water
8 tbsp soy yoghurt
5–6 tbsp fruit muesli/granola (rolled oats, mixed nuts, dried fruit, seeds)

Method:

1. Put the apples in a pan with the sugar and water. Cover the pan and heat gently until the sugar has dissolved.

2. Bring to a boil and cook, stirring occasionally for 5–8 minutes, until the apple slices break down and become fluffy. Add more sugar if required.

3. Spoon into serving glasses and spoon the yoghurt on top. Spoon the muesli or granola on top.

BANANA AND PECAN BREAD

Makes 1 cake
Preparation and cooking time 1 hour 20 minutes

Ingredients:

3 large very ripe bananas, mashed
75 ml | 2½ fl oz | ⅓ cup sunflower oil
100 g | 3½ oz | ½ cup light brown sugar
225 g | 8 oz | 2 cups self-raising flour
2 heaped tsp baking powder
3 tsp mixed spice
50 g | 1¾ oz | ½ cup chopped pecan nuts

Method:

1. Heat the oven to 180°C (160°C fan | 350°F | gas 4). Grease a 1 kg | 2 lb loaf tin.

2. Mix together the bananas, oil and sugar until blended.

3. Add the flour, baking powder and spice, and mix well. Stir in the pecans.

4. Spoon into the loaf tin and bake for about 60 minutes until golden and risen. Cover with foil if the cake is browning too quickly. Cool in the tin for 10 minutes, then turn out onto a wire rack to cool completely.

SCRAMBLED TOFU WITH VEGETABLES

Serves 4
Preparation and cooking time 20 minutes

Ingredients:

1 tbsp vegetable oil
2 zucchinis (courgettes), chopped
1 onion, chopped
2 tomatoes, chopped
1 clove garlic, finely chopped
400 g | 14 oz firm tofu, drained
1 tsp turmeric
salt and pepper
1 tbsp finely chopped parsley

Method:

1. Heat the oil in a shallow pan and cook the vegetables and garlic until they begin to soften.

2. Crumble in the tofu and add the turmeric.

3. Cook, stirring for 5–8 minutes until the vegetables are tender. Season to taste with salt and pepper.

4. Serve immediately, sprinkled with parsley.

BUCKWHEAT PANCAKES WITH BLUEBERRIES

Makes 10–12 pancakes
Preparation and cooking 25 minutes

Ingredients:

175 g | 6 oz | 1½ cups buckwheat flour
50 g | 1¾ oz | ½ cup oat bran
50 g | 1¾ oz | ½ cup wheat bran
1 tsp bicarbonate of (baking) soda
½ tsp salt
450 ml | 16 fl oz | 2 cups soy milk
vegetable oil, for cooking

To serve:
maple syrup
100 g | 3½ oz | 1 cup blueberries

Method:

1. Stir together the dry ingredients in a mixing bowl.

2. Add the soy milk and stir until thoroughly combined.

3. Brush a frying pan (skillet) with oil and heat until hot but not smoking. Working in batches, pour 55 ml | ¼ cup of batter for each pancake into the pan and cook until bubbles appear on the surface and the undersides are golden brown. Turn the pancakes over, then turn off the heat and let the pancakes continue to cook in the pan until the undersides are firm and golden brown.

4. Place on serving plates and drizzle with maple syrup. Sprinkle over the blueberries.

STRAWBERRY BANANA MUFFINS

Makes 12 muffins
Preparation and cooking time 45 minutes

Ingredients:

112 g | 4 oz | ½ cup soy yoghurt
2 very ripe bananas, mashed
1 tsp vanilla extract
112 g | 4 oz | ½ cup vegan margarine, melted
250 g | 9 oz | 2¼ cups plain (all-purpose) flour
175 g | 6 oz | ¾ cup white (granulated) sugar
1½ tsp baking powder
¼ tsp bicarbonate of (baking) soda
¼ tsp salt
200 g | 7 oz | 1 cup sliced strawberries

Method:

1. Heat the oven to 180°C (160°C fan | 350°F | gas 4). Place paper cases in a 12-hole muffin tin.

2. Stir together the yoghurt, mashed bananas and vanilla. Stir in the margarine.

3. Sift the dry ingredients into a mixing bowl and gently fold in the strawberries, making sure they are coated with flour.

4. Add the wet ingredients to the dry ingredients and stir until just combined.

5. Spoon the mixture into the paper cases. Bake for 20–25 minutes, until golden and risen. Place on a wire rack to cool completely.

HOMEMADE FRUIT, NUT AND SEED BARS

Makes 12 bars
Preparation and cooking 20 minutes

Ingredients:

110 g | 4 oz | 1 cup (heaped) rolled oats
175 g | 6 oz | ¾ cup vegan margarine
8 tbsp maple syrup
3 tbsp light brown sugar
100 g | 3½ oz | ⅔ cup hazelnuts, roughly chopped
100 g | 3½ oz | ⅔ cup Brazil nuts, roughly chopped
100 g | 3½ oz | ⅔ cup cashew nuts, roughly chopped
150 g | 5 oz | 1 cup chopped figs
150 g | 5 oz | 1 cup chopped prunes
50 g | 1¾ oz | ½ cup pumpkin seeds
125 g | 4½ oz | 1 cup sesame seeds

Method:

1. Grease and line a 20 cm | 8" square tin.

2. Toast the oats in a dry frying pan (skillet) until lightly browned.

3. Heat the margarine, maple syrup and sugar in a large pan until melted and the sugar has dissolved.

4. Stir the remaining ingredients into the pan. Mix well and pour into the tin. Press the mixture down and leave to cool, then slice into bars.

APPLE RÖSTI

Serves 4–6
Preparation and cooking 45 minutes

Ingredients:

300 g | 11 oz potatoes, unpeeled
2 firm apples
2 tbsp lemon juice
grated nutmeg
salt
freshly ground black pepper
2–3 tbsp vegetable oil

To garnish:
salad leaves
peppercorns, crushed
diced apple
black (ripe) olives, pitted

Method:

1. Put the potatoes in a pan and cover with water. Add a pinch of salt and bring to a boil. Cook for 6 minutes, then drain and set aside to cool.

2. Peel the apples and grate them coarsely into a large bowl. Add the lemon juice and toss well to coat.

3. Peel the potatoes and grate them coarsely into the bowl. Season with nutmeg and generously season with salt and pepper. Divide into 4–6 portions.

4. Heat some of the oil in a frying pan (skillet) and fry the rösti one at a time. Cook until golden brown on the base, then turn over and cook the other side until golden brown. Transfer to a plate and put in the oven to keep warm. Repeat with the remaining oil and potato mixture.

5. Serve garnished with salad leaves, crushed peppercorns, diced apple and olives.

BREAKFAST PARFAIT

Serves 4
Preparation and cooking 30 minutes

Ingredients:

100 g | 3½ oz | 1 cup blueberries
water
white (granulated) sugar, to taste
200 g | 7 oz | 2 cups rolled oats
85 g | 3 oz | 1 cup chopped nuts, almonds, walnuts or hazelnuts
250 g | 9 oz | 2 cups raspberries
icing (confectioner's) sugar, to taste
400 g | 14 oz soy yoghurt

Method:

1. Place the blueberries and white (granulated) sugar in a pan with just enough water to cover them. Warm over a medium heat until the sugar has dissolved. Bring to a boil, then reduce the heat and simmer gently until the blueberries have softened but are still whole. Set aside to cool completely.

2. Toast the oats and nuts in a dry frying pan (skillet) until lightly golden. Put into a bowl and set aside to cool.

3. Puree the raspberries in a blender and press through a sieve to remove the seeds. Sweeten to taste with icing (confectioner's) sugar. Set 4 tablespoons aside for the topping.

4. Stir half the oats and nuts into the larger amount of raspberry puree and divide between 4 serving glasses.

5. Spoon a layer of yoghurt on top. Cover with a layer of oats and nuts.

6. Add a spoonful of yoghurt and top with the reserved raspberry puree.

7. Spoon the blueberries on top and chill until ready to serve.

LUNCH

These healthy lunch recipes are a great way to pack more nutrients into your day. There are hearty lunches for the cooler months, lighter lunches for the warmer months and options that work well all year round.

POTATO AND CORN FRITTERS

Saves 4–6
Preparation and cooking 30 minutes

Ingredients:

400 g | 14 oz potatoes, coarsely grated
1 onion, grated
2 tbsp cornflour (cornstarch)
2–3 tbsp chopped parsley
400 g | 14 oz canned corn kernels (sweetcorn), drained
salt
freshly ground black pepper
vegetable oil, for frying

To garnish:
parsley

Method:

1. Dry the grated potatoes and onion in a tea towel – it's important to remove as much moisture as possible. Mix with the cornflour (cornstarch), parsley and corn kernels (sweetcorn) and season with salt and pepper.

2. Heat the oil in a large, heavy-based frying pan (skillet). Add mounds of the potato mixture, flatten the surface with a flat spatula, and cook over a medium-low heat for about 10 minutes until cooked and browned on the bases.

3. Turn each fritter carefully and cook the other side over a low heat for a further 10 minutes.

4. Serve garnished with parsley.

CELLOPHANE NOODLE SALAD

Serves 4
Preparation and cooking 25 minutes

Ingredients:

200 g | 7 oz cellophane (vermicelli) noodles
12 green asparagus spears, trimmed
3 tbsp vegetable oil
1 lime, juice
1 tbsp light soy sauce
1 tsp white (granulated) sugar
1 red chilli deseeded and sliced
salt
1 red capsicum (pepper), deseeded and sliced
1 orange capsicum (pepper), deseeded and sliced
1 tbsp black onion seeds

Method:

1. Soak the noodles in boiling water according to the packet instructions. Drain, refresh in cold water and set aside in a large bowl.

2. Blanch the asparagus in boiling salted water, drain, refresh in cold water then cut into 5 cm | 2" lengths and add to the noodles.

3. Mix together the oil, lime juice, soy sauce, sugar and chilli and season to taste with salt.

4. Mix the sliced capsicums (peppers) into the noodles, stir in the dressing and scatter over the black onion seeds.

Tip: Cellophane noodles can be found in Asian food stores and some supermarkets.

COUSCOUS CAKES

Serves 4
Preparation and cooking 50 minutes

Ingredients:

250 g | 9 oz | 1¾ cups couscous
250 ml | 9 fl oz | 1 cup boiling vegetable stock (broth)
2 tbsp vegetable oil
1 small turnip, grated
1 carrot, grated
1 small onion, finely chopped
salt, to taste
freshly ground pepper, to taste
1 tsp grated lemon zest
1 tsp cumin seeds
1 tsp turmeric
1 pinch ground coriander
1–2 tbsp tahini
2–3 tbsp flour

For the cucumber sprout salad:
2 cucumbers, thinly sliced
150 g | 5 oz lentil sprouts
30 ml | 1 fl oz | ⅛ cup white wine vinegar
2 tbsp lemon juice
3 tbsp olive oil
salt
freshly ground pepper

Method:

1. Pour the couscous in a bowl and pour over the stock (broth). Leave to swell for 20 minutes, then break up with a fork.

2. Heat the oven to 180°C (160°C fan | 350°F | gas 4). Line a large baking tray (sheet) with non-stick baking paper.

3. Heat the oil in a frying pan (skillet) and cook the turnip, carrot and onion until soft, then remove from the heat.

4. Stir into the couscous with the salt, pepper, lemon zest, cumin, turmeric, coriander and tahini. Stir in the flour until a pliable dough is formed.

5. Shape the couscous dough into small patties and place on the baking tray.

6. Bake for 15–20 minutes until golden.

7. For the cucumber sprout salad: mix the cucumber with the sprouts.

8. Whisk together the vinegar, lemon juice and oil and toss with the cucumber and sprouts. Season with salt and pepper.

CAPONATA

Serves 4
Preparation and cooking 50 minutes

Ingredients:

4 tbsp olive oil
2 eggplants (aubergines), chopped
2 red capsicums (peppers), chopped
3–4 zucchinis (courgettes), chopped
1 onion, chopped
salt
freshly ground black pepper
3 tbsp capers, rinsed and drained
2 tbsp red wine vinegar
1½ tbsp white (granulated) sugar
extra virgin olive oil, for drizzling

To garnish:
flat-leaf parsley, torn into strips

To serve:
toasted crusty bread

Method:

1. Heat half the olive oil in a large frying pan (skillet) and cook the eggplants (aubergines) for about 10 minutes until browned. Remove from the pan and set aside.

2. Heat the remaining olive oil in the pan and cook the capsicums (peppers) and zucchinis (courgettes) until beginning to soften. Add the onion and season with salt and pepper. Cook gently for 15–20 minutes until the vegetables are tender.

3. Add the cooled eggplant and capers to the pan.

4. Mix together the vinegar and sugar. Add to the pan and cook for 10 minutes, stirring.

5. Put into a serving bowl and garnish with parsley. Drizzle with extra virgin olive oil. Serve hot or cold with toasted crusty bread.

FALAFEL WRAPS

Serves 8
Preparation and cooking 30 minutes

Ingredients:

800 g | 28 oz canned chickpeas (garbanzo beans),
  rinsed and drained
2 cloves garlic, finely chopped
1 small onion, finely chopped
2 tsp ground cumin
2 tsp ground coriander
1 handful fresh coriander (cilantro), leaves chopped
1 tsp harissa paste
4 tbsp plain (all-purpose) flour
½ tsp salt
7–8 tbsp sesame seeds
4–5 tbsp sunflower oil

To serve:
chopped tomatoes
salad leaves
flour tortillas or wraps
soy yoghurt

Method:

1. Put all the ingredients except the sesame seeds and oil into a food processor or blender and blend until fairly smooth. Shape into 8 balls.

2. Sprinkle the sesame seeds onto a plate and roll the balls in the sesame seeds to coat. Flatten the balls slightly.

3. Heat the oil in a large frying pan (skillet), and cook the falafel, 2–3 at a time, for 3 minutes on each side until lightly golden.

4. Drain on absorbent kitchen paper and serve with chopped tomatoes, salad leaves, flour tortillas or wraps, and yoghurt.

MEXICAN QUINOA SALAD

Serves 4–6
Preparation and cooking 55 minutes

Ingredients:

180 g | 6 oz | 1 cup quinoa, rinsed
340 ml | 12 fl oz | 1½ cups water
salt
2 tsp vegetable oil
1 jalapeno chilli, seeds removed, finely chopped
2 cloves garlic, crushed
1 small red capsicum (pepper), diced
1 small green capsicum (pepper), diced
1 tsp ground cumin
1 tsp ground coriander
2 limes, juice

2–4 tbsp extra virgin olive oil
100–200 g | 3½–7 oz canned black beans, drained and rinsed
2 large ripe tomatoes, diced
½ small cucumber, chopped
200 g | 7 oz canned corn (sweetcorn) kernels, drained
3 tbsp chopped coriander (cilantro)
4 spring (green) onions, chopped
1 avocado
2 tsp lemon juice
freshly ground pepper

Method:

1. Put the quinoa, water and ¼ teaspoon of salt into a pan. Cover and bring to a boil.

2. Reduce the heat and simmer for about 15 minutes, until the water has evaporated. Remove from the heat and stand for 5 minutes with the lid on. Fluff the quinoa gently with a fork and put into a bowl.

3. Heat the vegetable oil in a frying pan (skillet) and gently cook the jalapeno and garlic until softened but not browned.

4. Add the capsicums (peppers) and cook for 5 minutes.

5. Add the cumin and coriander and cook, stirring for 2 minutes.

6. Whisk together the lime juice, olive oil and ½ teaspoon of salt and set aside.

7. Combine the quinoa, black beans, cooked vegetables, tomatoes, cucumber, corn kernels (sweetcorn), fresh coriander (cilantro) and spring (green) onions in a large bowl.

8. Peel the avocado and dice the flesh. Toss in the lemon juice, then add to the quinoa mixture.

9. Pour on the lime juice mixture and stir gently to combine. Season to taste with salt and pepper.

CHILLI CORN SOUP

Serves 4
Preparation and cooking 35 minutes

Ingredients:

2 tbsp olive oil
2 onions, thinly sliced
3 cloves garlic, crushed
1 tbsp coriander seeds, crushed
5 cobs corn (sweetcorn) kernels
1 green chilli, finely chopped
vegetable stock (broth)
salt and pepper

To garnish:
torn coriander (cilantro)
lemon wedges

Method:

1. Heat the oil in a pan and cook the onion until softened. Add the garlic, coriander seeds and corn (sweetcorn) kernels and continue to cook for another 5 minutes.

2. Add the chilli and enough stock (broth) to just cover. Season to taste and simmer for about 20 minutes. Remove from the heat and cool slightly.

3. Ladle half the mixture into a blender or food processor and blend until smooth.

4. Combine smooth and chunky halves and return to the pan and reheat, stirring, until piping hot.

5. Pour into warm serving bowls and garnish with coriander (cilantro) and lemon wedges.

WILD RICE SALAD

Serves 4
Preparation and cooking 1 hour

Ingredients:

450 ml | 16 fl oz | 2 cups water
85 g | 3 oz | ½ cup wild rice, well rinsed
salt
225 g | 8 oz | 1 cup long grain white rice
100 g | 3½ oz | 1 cup chopped wild mushrooms
1 onion, diced
330 ml | 12 fl oz | 1⅓ cups vegetable stock (broth)
450 g | 16 oz asparagus, chopped
1 tbsp extra virgin olive oil
1½ tbsp balsamic vinegar
1 tsp lemon juice
1 tbsp chopped coriander (cilantro)
freshly ground pepper, to taste
1 carrot, grated

Method:

1. Put the water, wild rice and 1 teaspoon of salt in a pan and bring to a boil. Reduce the heat and cover the pan. Simmer for 30–35 minutes until tender. Add the white rice for the last 15 minutes. Drain well.

2. Heat the mushrooms, onion and half the stock (broth) in a large frying pan (skillet) and simmer for about 10 minutes until the mushrooms are cooked and browned.

3. Add the asparagus and the remaining stock and cook for a few minutes, until the asparagus is slightly soft.

4. Whisk together the olive oil, balsamic vinegar and lemon juice.

5. Toss together the rice, vegetables, olive oil mixture and coriander (cilantro), stirring to thoroughly combine. Season generously with salt and pepper.

6. Sprinkle with the grated carrot and serve hot or cold.

DINNER

Try these recipes for healthy dinners that are full of colour, flavour and nutritious ingredients. They are easy to prepare for everyday dinners but impressive enough for entertaining.

RUSTIC TOMATO PIZZA

Serves 4
Preparation and cooking 50 minutes

Ingredients:

For the base:
300 g | 11 oz | 2¾ cups bread (strong) flour, plus extra for dusting
1 tsp fast-action dried yeast
1 tsp salt
200 ml | 7 fl oz | ⅞ cup warm water
1 tbsp olive oil, plus extra for drizzling

For the topping:
3–4 tbsp vegan pesto
200 g | 7 oz cherry tomatoes, red and yellow
200 g | 7 oz roma (plum) tomatoes, sliced
salt
freshly ground black pepper

To garnish:
purple or regular thyme

Method:

1. For the base: mix together the flour, yeast and salt in a mixing bowl. Make a well in the centre and pour in the water and oil. Mix to a soft, fairly wet dough.

2. Turn onto a lightly floured surface and knead for 5 minutes until smooth. Put into a lightly greased bowl, cover with a tea towel and leave to rise until doubled in size – about 1 hour.

3. Heat the oven to 200°C (180°C fan | 400°F | gas 6). Line a baking tray (sheet) with non-stick baking paper.

4. Quickly knead the dough and roll out into a large oval about 25 cm | 10" in diameter. Place on the baking tray.

5. For the topping: brush the dough with pesto.

6. Cut some of the cherry tomatoes in half and leave the rest whole. Place all the tomatoes on the base and season with salt and pepper.

7. Drizzle with oil and bake for about 20 minutes until the base is cooked and the tomatoes are tender. Garnish with thyme.

RICE AND VEGETABLE PAELLA

Serves 4
Preparation and cooking 50 minutes

Ingredients:

2½ tbsp olive oil

2 cloves garlic, crushed

1 large onion, finely chopped

1 stick celery, finely chopped

2 firm tomatoes, peeled and chopped

100 ml | 3½ fl oz | 7 tbsp boiling water

½ tsp saffron threads

300 g | 11 oz | 1¾ cups Calasparra or paella rice, rinsed and drained

1 tsp paprika

700–800 ml | 25–28 fl oz | 3–3½ cups vegetable stock (broth)

1 large carrot, diced

225 g | 8 oz green beans, trimmed chopped to 1 cm (½") lengths

1 red capsicum (pepper), seeds removed, diced

150 g | 5 oz | 1 cup peas

salt and pepper

180 g | 6 oz | 1 cup black (ripe) olives, pitted

Method:

1. Heat 2 tablespoons olive oil in paella pan. Add the garlic and cook for 1 minute, then add the onion and celery. Cook gently until softened, then add the tomatoes and cook for 5 minutes.

2. Add the saffron to the boiling water and stir well, then add to the pan and simmer for 3 minutes.

3. Add the rinsed rice to the pan with the paprika, stock (broth), saffron water and saffron threads. Bring to a simmer and cook for 10 minutes.

4. Stir the rice and add the chopped carrots, green beans and red capsicum (pepper). Cook for 20 minutes, then stir in the peas and continue cooking, stirring occasionally, until the rice is tender and the stock absorbed. Add a little more stock or water if the mixture is too dry. Season to taste with salt and pepper and stir in the olives.

VEGETABLE STEW WITH DUMPLINGS

Serves 4
Preparation and cooking 1 hour 10 minutes

Ingredients:

1 tbsp olive oil
1 onion, chopped
½ tsp salt
½ tsp freshly ground black pepper
1 bay leaf
½ tsp dried thyme
450 g | 16 oz | 2 cups canned chopped tomatoes
900 ml | 32 fl oz | 4 cups vegetable stock (broth)
50 g | 1¾ oz | ¼ cup pearl barley
1 butternut pumpkin (squash), cubed
1 small sweet potato (yam), cubed

For the dumplings:
200 g | 7 oz | 1¾ cups self-raising flour, plus extra for rolling
100 g | 3½ oz | ¾ cup shredded vegetarian suet or vegan margarine
salt and pepper
2 tbsp vegan pesto
water

Method:

1. Heat the oil in a pan and cook the onion for 5 minutes until softened.

2. Add the salt, pepper, bay leaf, thyme, tomatoes and stock (broth). Bring to a boil and stir in the barley. Reduce the heat, cover and simmer for 30 minutes.

3. For the dumplings: mix the flour and suet or margarine in a mixing bowl. Season with salt and pepper. Stir in the pesto and just enough water to form a soft dough. Roll into small balls with floured hands. Set aside.

4. Add the pumpkin (squash) and sweet potato (yam) to the pan and return to a boil. Add the dumplings, reduce the heat, cover and simmer for 15–20 minutes until the vegetables are tender and the dumplings are cooked.

STUFFED TOMATOES

Serves 4
Preparation and cooking 50 minutes

Ingredients:

150 g | 5 oz | ⅔ cup white long grain rice
300 ml | 11 fl oz | 1⅓ cups water
salt
8 tomatoes
olive oil
1 clove garlic
1 shallot
1 tbsp chopped fresh parsley
1 red capsicum (pepper), seeds removed, diced
1 tbsp tomato paste (puree)
freshly ground black pepper
100 ml | 3½ fl oz | 7 tbsp vegetable stock (broth)

Method:

1. Put the rice in a pan with the water and salt and bring to a boil. Cover and cook gently until the rice is cooked and the water is absorbed.

2. Heat the oven to 200°C (180°C fan | 400°F | gas 6). Grease a baking dish.

3. Cut the tops off the tomatoes and scoop out the flesh.

4. Heat the oil in a pan and cook the garlic and shallot until soft. Remove from the heat and stir in the parsley. Set aside to cool.

5. Mix the diced capsicum (pepper) with the rice, shallots, garlic and tomato paste (puree). Season to taste with salt and pepper.

6. Place the tomatoes in the baking dish and fill with the rice mixture. Replace the tops and drizzle with a little olive oil. Pour in the stock (broth).

7. Bake for about 20 minutes until tender and piping hot. Serve immediately.

RISOTTO WITH GREEN VEGETABLES

Serves 4
Preparation and cooking 35 minutes

Ingredients:

2 tbsp olive oil

2 shallots, finely chopped

200 g | 7 oz | 1 cup risotto rice

850 ml | 30 fl oz | 3½ cups hot vegetable stock (broth)

300 g | 11 oz | 2 cups frozen peas

2 tbsp chopped mint

50 g | 1¾ oz | ½ cup grated vegan cheese

salt and pepper

12 runner (pole) beans or green beans, sliced diagonally and steamed

1 bunch asparagus, trimmed and steamed

Method:

1. Heat the oil in a wide pan and cook the shallots very gently until soft but not brown.

2. Add the rice and stir until the rice becomes translucent, then add a ladle of stock (broth) and stir until it is absorbed by the rice. Reduce the heat and continue adding the stock one ladle at a time, stirring constantly until the rice has become creamy and just cooked through. You may need to add a little more stock or water.

3. Add the peas, mint and cheese, season with salt and pepper and continue cooking until the peas are cooked through.

4. Serve topped with the beans and asparagus.

VEGAN SHEPHERD'S PIE

Serves 4
Preparation and cooking 1 hour 30 minutes

Ingredients:

300 g | 11 oz | ¾ pound floury potatoes
2 tbsp vegetable oil
1 onion, finely chopped
1 carrot, finely chopped
1 red capsicum (pepper), deseeded and chopped
1 tbsp flour
250 ml | 9 fl oz | 1 cup vegetable stock (broth) or water
100 g | 3½ oz | 1 cup peas, frozen
200 g | 7 oz | 1 cup canned green lentils, rinsed and drained
salt and pepper
75–100 ml | 2½–3½ fl oz | 5–7 tbsp olive oil
grated nutmeg

Method:

1. Heat the oven to 200°C (180°C fan | 400°F | gas 6). Grease 4 pie dishes.

2. Cook the potatoes in boiling salted water for about 25 minutes until soft.

3. Heat the vegetable oil and cook the onions for 5 minutes, then add the carrots and capsicum (pepper) and cook until the vegetables are tender.

4. Dust with the flour and add the vegetable stock (broth). Bring to a boil, stir in the peas and lentils and season with salt and pepper.

5. Drain and mash the potatoes, stir in the olive oil and season with salt, pepper and nutmeg.

6. Spoon the lentil mixture into the dishes and top with mashed potato.

7. Bake for 30 minutes until golden brown.

RICE NOODLE SALAD WITH TOFU

Serves 4
Preparation and cooking 25 minutes + standing 1 hour

Ingredients:

3 tbsp rice vinegar
2 tbsp miso
1 tbsp grated ginger (gingerroot)
1 tbsp soy sauce
1½ tbsp light brown sugar
1 tbsp sesame oil
400 g | 14 oz extra-firm tofu
120 g | 4 oz flat rice noodles
2 tbsp vegetable oil
2 cloves garlic, finely chopped
1 red chilli, seeds removed, finely chopped
3–4 spring (green) onions, chopped

To garnish:
lime wedges
torn coriander (cilantro) leaves

Method:

1. Whisk together the rice vinegar, miso, ginger (gingerroot), soy sauce, sugar and sesame oil and set aside.

2. Drain the tofu and pat dry. Cut into pieces and add to the rice vinegar mixture. Stir and leave to stand for at least 1 hour, then remove tofu from mixture and set aside.

3. Cook or soak the noodles according to the directions on the packet, then drain and rinse.

4. Combine the noodles with the rice vinegar mixture in a serving bowl and toss to coat.

5. Heat half the vegetable oil in a frying pan (skillet) and add the tofu. Cook for 3 minutes on each side, until browned and crisp. Remove from the pan.

6. Heat the remaining vegetable oil in the pan and cook the garlic, chilli and spring (green) onions for 3–4 minutes, until tender.

7. Toss the noodles with the tofu and the contents of the pan, and place on warm serving plates. Garnish with lime wedges and sprinkle with coriander (cilantro).

ROOT VEGETABLE CURRY

Serves 4
Preparation and cooking 1 hour 25 minutes

Ingredients:

1 tbsp olive oil
1–2 chillies, finely chopped
50 g | 1¾ oz Thai curry paste
750 g | 26 oz mixed root vegetables: carrot, swede,
   potatoes, chopped
water
160 ml | 6 fl oz | ⅔ cup coconut cream
750 m vegetable stock (broth)
salt
freshly ground black pepper
1 tbsp chopped Thai basil

For the barley:
500 ml | 18 fl oz | 2 cups vegetable stock
200 g | 7 oz pearl barley
salt
freshly ground black pepper

To garnish:
Thai basil

Method:

1. Heat the oil in a wide shallow pan and cook the chillies for 30 seconds. Add the curry paste and cook, stirring for 2 minutes.

2. Add the vegetables and stir, coating the vegetables in the paste. Add a little water to help stop the vegetables from sticking. Cover and cook for 10 minutes, stirring occasionally.

3. Mix together the coconut cream and stock (broth) and pour into the pan.

4. Simmer uncovered, for about 30 minutes, until the vegetables are soft. Season to taste with salt and pepper and stir in the Thai basil.

5. For the barley: heat the stock in a pan until boiling. Add the barley and return to a boil, stirring constantly. Cover and simmer very gently for about 20 minutes, until all the stock is absorbed.

6. Remove from the heat and season with salt and pepper.

7. Ladle the curry into warm bowls and spoon the barley on top. Garnish with torn Thai basil.

DESSERT

Choosing a vegan diet doesn't mean you have to deny yourself dessert. These delicious dessert recipes use vegan alternatives, such as soy milk and vegan chocolate, so you can still enjoy some sweetness in your life.

STRAWBERRY MOUSSE

Serves 4–6
Preparation and cooking 20 minutes + chilling 1 hour

Ingredients:

400 g | 14 oz | 2 cups sliced strawberries
400 g | 14 oz | 2 cups firm silken tofu, drained
3 tbsp agave syrup

To decorate:
strawberries

Method:

1. Puree the strawberries in a blender or food processor until smooth. Press through a sieve to remove the seeds, then return the puree to the food processor.

2. Gradually add the tofu, a little at a time and blend until incorporated. Add the agave syrup and process for 1–2 minutes until light and creamy.

3. Spoon into serving bowls and chill for at least 1 hour until firm. Decorate with strawberries.

WALNUT BROWNIE BARS

Makes 12 bars
Preparation and cooking 1 hour 15 minutes + cooling 30 minutes

Ingredients:

350 g | 12 oz extra firm silken tofu
255 g | 9 oz | 2¼ cups plain (all-purpose) flour
150 ml | 5 fl oz | ⅔ cup water
175 g | 6 oz dark (semisweet) vegan chocolate, 70% cocoa solids, chopped
400 g | 14 oz | 1¾ cups white (granulated) sugar
¼ tsp salt
2 tsp vanilla extract
110 ml | 4 fl oz | 7 tbsp sunflower oil
75 g | 2½ oz | ¾ cup cocoa powder
75 g | 2½ oz | ½ cup chopped walnuts

Method:

1. Heat the oven to 180°C (160°C fan | 350°F | gas 4). Grease an 18 x 28 cm | 7" x 11" baking tin and line the base with non-stick baking paper.

2. Puree the tofu, 75 g | 2 ½ oz flour and water in a blender or food processor until smooth. Pour into a pan and whisk constantly over a low heat until thickened. Do not boil.

3. Remove from the heat and stir in the chocolate, sugar, salt and vanilla until the chocolate has melted. Set aside to cool for 30 minutes.

4. Stir in the oil until smooth, then stir in the cocoa, remaining flour and walnuts until blended.

5. Put into the tin and spread evenly. Bake for 35–40 minutes until cooked, but the centre is still a little soft to the touch. Cool in the tin.

6. Cut into bars to serve.

ORANGE AND POPPY SEED CAKE

Makes 1 cake
Preparation and cooking 1 hour 40 minutes

Ingredients:

For the caramelised orange slices:
400 ml | 14 fl oz | 1⅔ cups water
350 g | 12 oz | 1½ cups white (granulated) sugar
2–3 unwaxed oranges, very thinly sliced

For the cake batter:
225 g | 8 oz | 2 cups self-raising flour
50 g | 1¾ oz | ¼ cup vegan margarine, softened
225 g | 8 oz | 1 cup caster (superfine) sugar
225 ml | 8 fl oz | 1 cup soy milk
50 ml | 1¾ fl oz | 10 tsp orange juice
1 tsp vanilla extract
2½ tbsp poppy seeds
1 tsp finely grated orange zest

Method:

1. For the caramelised orange slices: heat the water and sugar in a pan over a low heat until the sugar has dissolved completely. Add the orange slices and bring to a boil. Reduce the heat, cover and simmer for about 20 minutes, until the oranges are tender. Drain and set aside.

2. For the cake batter: heat the oven to 180°C (160°C fan | 350°F | gas 4). Grease a 20 cm | 8" diameter cake tin.

3. Press the orange slices into the tin onto the base and sides, overlapping them slightly.

4. Put the flour, margarine, sugar, soy milk, orange juice and vanilla into a mixing bowl. Beat for 1 minute with an electric whisk until creamy.

5. Stir in the poppy seeds and orange zest and mix well.

6. Put into the tin and bake for 50–55 minutes until golden brown and springy to the touch. Test by inserting a skewer or cocktail stick into the centre of the cake – if it comes out clean the cake is cooked.

7. Remove from the oven and leave to cool in the tin. Turn the cake out so the orange slices are uppermost.

WATERMELON GRANITA

Serves 4
Preparation and cooking 20 minutes + freezing 4 hours

Ingredients:

500 g | 18 oz watermelon flesh
1 pinch salt
1 lime, juice
25 g | 1 oz | ⅛ cup caster (superfine) sugar

To decorate:
mint leaves

Method:

1. Put the watermelon flesh, salt and lime juice in a food processor or blender and blend until combined.

2. Push the mixture through a fine sieve into a freezerproof container. Stir in the sugar until dissolved.

3. Freeze for 1 hour, then mix the granita with a fork. Return to the freezer and freeze for a further hour. Continue this twice more until the mixture is completely frozen. Once frozen, scrape with a fork to form fluffy ice and spoon into small glasses.

4. Decorate with mint leaves.

CHURROS WITH CHOCOLATE DIP

Serves 4
Preparation and cooking 40 minutes

Ingredients:

225 ml | 8 fl oz | 1 cup water
2½ tbsp white (granulated) sugar
½ tsp salt
110 g | 4 oz | 1 cup plain (all-purpose) flour
few drops vanilla extract
sunflower oil, for deep frying

For the sauce:
175 g | 6 oz | 1 cup chopped vegan dark (semisweet)
    chocolate, 70% cocoa solids
110 ml | 4 fl oz | 7 tbsp rice or soy milk
1 tsp vegan margarine

Method:

1. Put the water, sugar and salt into a pan and bring to a boil, stirring.

2. Remove from the heat, add the flour all at once and the vanilla and beat until smooth.

3. Heat the oil in a deep-fat fryer or deep heavy-based pan.

4. Spoon the churro mixture into a piping bag fitted with a fluted nozzle. Pipe 7½ cm | 3" lengths of dough directly into the hot oil and cook for 3–4 minutes until golden, turning once. Do this in batches as it is important not to overcrowd the pan. Drain on absorbent kitchen paper.

5. For the sauce: put all the ingredients into a pan and heat gently until the chocolate has melted. Stir and serve with the churros.

CHOCOLATE CHILLI DOUGHNUTS

Makes 12 doughnuts
Preparation and cooking 1 hour

Ingredients:

75 g | 2½ oz | ½ cup oat flour
75 g | 2½ oz | ½ cup sweet rice flour
110 g | 4 oz | ½ cup white (granulated) sugar
25 g | 1 oz | ¼ cup cocoa powder
2 tbsp ground almonds
2 tbsp coconut flour
2 tbsp ground flax seeds
1 tsp gluten-free baking powder
½ tsp bicarbonate of (baking) soda
½–1 tsp chilli powder
½ tsp salt
175 ml | 6 fl oz | ¾ cup almond milk
55 ml | 2 fl oz | 11 tsp unsweetened apple sauce
3 tbsp sunflower oil
80 g | 3 oz | ½ cup vegan chocolate chips

To decorate:
200 ml | 7 fl oz | ⅞ cup coconut milk
250 g | 9 oz dark (semisweet) dairy-free chocolate, chopped
vanilla-infused coarse sea salt

Method:

1. Heat the oven to 170°C (150°C fan | 335°F | gas 3). Grease 12 doughnut tins.

2. Mix together the dry ingredients in a mixing bowl until combined.

3. Add the wet ingredients and mix until just combined. Leave to stand for 5 minutes.

4. Spoon into the tins and lightly smooth the tops with wet fingers.

5. Bake for 18–23 minutes, until firm to the touch. Cool in the tins for 2 minutes, then place on a wire rack to cool completely.

6. To decorate: heat the coconut milk until bubbles begin to appear around the edges. Pour over the chopped chocolate and stand without stirring for 5 minutes.

7. After 5 minutes, stir until smooth. Leave to cool and thicken slightly.

8. Spoon over the doughnuts and sprinkle lightly with vanilla-infused coarse sea salt. Leave to set.

PANNA COTTA WITH BERRY AND CHERRY SAUCE

Serves 4
Preparation and cooking 20 minutes

Ingredients:

2 tbsp agar agar flakes or 2 tsp agar agar powder
100 ml | 3½ fl oz | 7 tbsp water
450 ml | 16 fl oz | 2 cups almond milk
3–4 tbsp white (granulated) sugar

For the sauce:
110–120 ml | 4–4¼ fl oz | 7–8 tbsp juice, from the canned cherries
55 g | 2 oz | ¼ cup white sugar
2 tbsp cornflour (cornstarch)
½ tbsp lemon juice
200 g | 7 oz canned red cherries in juice
125 g | 4½ oz | 1 cup raspberries, crushed

Method:

1. Dissolve the agar agar in the water in a pan and bring to a boil, stirring constantly with a wooden spoon. Reduce the heat and stir for about 5 minutes.

2. Heat the almond milk, agar agar solution and sugar in a pan and stir occasionally until the agar agar has dissolved completely.

3. Pour into 4 ramekins or serving bowls and leave to set.

4. Heat the cherry juice in a pan and bring to a boil. Remove from the heat and whisk in the sugar, cornflour (cornstarch) and lemon juice. Cook for 1–2 minutes until thickened.

5. Add the cherries and raspberries and cook for 1 minute. Leave to cool.

6. Spoon on top of the panna cotta and leave until cold.

Tip: Test a small amount of the agar agar solution in a cold bowl – it should set in 20–30 seconds; if not, you may need more agar agar. If too firm add more water.

APPLE CRUMBLES

Serves 4
Preparation and cooking 50 minutes

Ingredients:

2 cooking apples, peeled, cored and diced
4 tbsp raisins
1 tbsp lemon juice
2 tsp ground cinnamon
1 tbsp caster (superfine) sugar
75 g | 2½ oz | ⅓ cup vegan margarine
150 g | 5 oz | 1¼ cup plain (all-purpose) flour
100 g | 3½ oz | ½ cup white (granulated) sugar
1 pinch salt
75 g | 2½ oz | 1 cup chopped almonds

Method:

1. Heat the oven to 190°C (170°C fan | 375°F | gas 5). Grease 4 individual baking dishes.

2. Toss the apples and raisins in the lemon juice, cinnamon and caster (superfine) sugar and divide between the baking dishes.

3. Put the margarine, flour, sugar and salt into a mixing bowl and rub together with your fingertips until the mixture resembles breadcrumbs. Stir in the almonds until combined.

4. Scatter handfuls of the crumble mixture over the top of the apples, pressing down lightly.

5. Bake for 20–25 minutes until the apples are tender.

DRINKS

These drink recipes include refreshing Iced Berry Mocktails, delicious Vanilla Macchiatos, spicy Chai Lattes and a range of colourful shakes, slushies and smoothies. Enjoy these blends of fresh vegan ingredients and drink your way to good health.

HEALTHY SHAKES

Serves 4
Preparation and cooking 10 minutes

Ingredients:

150 g | 5 oz soy yoghurt
2 very ripe bananas
300 g | 11 oz strawberries and raspberries, mixed
300 ml | 11 fl oz coconut or soy milk

To decorate:
blueberries

Method:

1. Put all the ingredients in a food processor and blend until smooth.

2. Pour into chilled glasses and decorate with blueberries.

MELON CUCUMBER SLUSHIES

Serves 4
Preparation and cooking 15 minutes

Ingredients:

700–800 g | 25–28 oz melon flesh, seeds removed, cubed
1 small cucumber, peeled, seeds removed and cut into chunks
white (granulated) sugar, to taste
1–2 tbsp lime juice
1 pinch salt
750 ml–1 l | 25–33 fl oz | 3–4 cups ice

To decorate:
melon balls

Method:

1. Combine the first 5 ingredients in a blender or food processor until smooth.

2. Add the ice and blend until smooth and slushy – making it as thin or as thick as you like. Decorate with melon balls and serve immediately.

VANILLA MACCHIATOS

Serves 4–6
Preparation and cooking 20 minutes + chilling 1 hour

Ingredients:

450 ml | 16 fl oz | 2 cups water
335 g | 12 oz | 1½ cups white (granulated) sugar
1 teaspoon vanilla extract
450–550 ml | 16–19 fl oz | 2–2⅓ cups soy milk
450 ml | 16 fl oz | 2 cups cold espresso coffee

Method:

1. Heat the water and sugar in a pan until the sugar has dissolved. Bring to a boil and boil for 5 minutes. Remove from the heat, cool and stir in the vanilla extract. Stir well and chill.

2. Pour some of the milk into chilled glasses and carefully spoon the vanilla syrup on top.

3. Pour the espresso on top and add some of the remaining milk.

4. Heat the last of the milk until hot, but not boiling, then pour into a food processor or blender. Blend until frothy. Alternatively, steam the milk using an electric milk frother.

5. Spoon the froth on top of the glasses and serve immediately.

ICED BERRY MOCKTAILS

Serves 4
Preparation and cooking 30 minutes

Ingredients:

150 g | 5 oz strawberries, hulled and roughly chopped
4 tbsp white (granulated) sugar
12 raspberries
12 blackberries
crushed ice
still or sparkling water

Method:

1. Put the strawberries and sugar in a small pan and heat gently until the strawberry juice begins to run and the sugar has dissolved. Pass the mixture through a fine sieve and let the juice cool.

2. Divide the raspberries and blackberries between 4 glasses and gently crush them with the handle of a wooden spoon.

3. Add the strawberry juice, fill the glasses with crushed ice and top with still or sparkling water. Stir well and serve.

MANGO BANANA MILKSHAKES

Serves 4
Preparation and cooking 15 minutes

Ingredients:

3 medium bananas, cut into chunks
3 ripe mangoes, peeled and chopped
450–550 ml | 16–19 fl oz | 2–2⅓ cups coconut or almond milk
white (granulated) sugar, to taste

Method:

1. Puree the banana and mango in a blender in a food processor.

2. Add the milk and process until smooth. Add more milk if it is too thick.

3. Add sugar to taste and pour into chilled glasses. Serve immediately.

BLUEBERRY AND REDCURRANT SMOOTHIES

Serves 4
Preparation and cooking 15 minutes

Ingredients:

250 ml | 9 fl oz | 1 cup almond mlk
250 g | 9 oz | 1 cup soy yoghurt
125 g | 4½ oz blueberries
125 g | 4½ oz redcurrants
1 large banana, cut into chunks
2 tbsp chopped almonds

Method:

1. Put all the ingredients in a food processor or blender and blend until smooth.

2. Pour into chilled glasses and sprinkle with chopped almonds.

CHAI LATTES

Serves 4
Preparation and cooking 20 minutes

Ingredients:

450 ml | 16 fl oz | 2 cups soy milk
4 cloves
5 cardamom pods, crushed
2 cinnamon sticks, broken
white (granulated) sugar, to taste
2 tbsp black tea leaves
1 tsp ground ginger

To decorate:
ground cinnamon

Method:

1. Pour the milk into a pan and add the cloves, cardamom pods, cinnamon sticks, sugar, tea leaves and ginger.

2. Heat gently and bring to a simmer. Simmer gently for 10 minutes.

3. Strain into a jug and, using an electric milk frother, steam the milk until thick and foamy.

4. Pour into glasses and spoon the foam on top. Sprinkle with ground cinnamon.

FROZEN LEMONADE

Serves 4
Preparation and cooking 10 minutes + freezing 16 hours

Ingredients:

560 ml | 20 fl oz | 2½ cups water, approx
110 g | 4 oz | ½ cup white (granulated) sugar, approx
340 ml | 12 fl oz | 1½ cups lemon juice

To decorate:
lemon slices

Method:

1. Combine 110 ml | ½ cup of water and the sugar in a pan. Heat just until the sugar dissolves, then set aside to cool.

2. Add the remaining water and 50 ml | ¼ cup of the sugar syrup to the lemon juice. Add more water or sugar syrup to taste. Once frozen, the lemonade will taste less sweet than it does at room temperature.

3. Pour the lemonade into a shallow freezerproof container. Cover and freeze, stirring with a fork every hour for the first 4 hours to break up the big ice crystals. Freeze overnight.

4. Scrape the tines of a fork across the surface of the frozen lemonade and scoop into glasses. Decorate with lemon slices and serve immediately.

WEIGHTS AND MEASURES

Weights and measures differ from country to country, but with these handy conversion charts cooking has never been easier!

Cup Measurements

One cup of these commonly used vegan ingredients is equal to the following weights.

Ingredient	Metric	Imperial
Apples (dried and chopped)	125 g	4½ oz
Apricots (dried and chopped)	190 g	6¾ oz
Breadcrumbs (packet)	125 g	4½ oz
Breadcrumbs (soft)	55 g	2 oz
Coconut (desiccated/fine)	90 g	3 oz
Flour (plain/all-purpose, self-raising)	115 g	4 oz
Fruit (dried)	170 g	6 oz
Golden syrup (golden corn syrup)	315 g	11 oz
Nuts (chopped)	115 g	4 oz
Rice (cooked)	155 g	5½ oz
Rice (uncooked)	225 g	8 oz
Sugar (brown)	155 g	5½ oz
Sugar (caster/superfine)	225 g	8 oz
Sugar (white/granulated)	225 g	8 oz
Sugar (sifted, icing/confectioner's)	155 g	5½ oz
Treacle (molasses)	315 g	11 oz
Vegan cheese (shredded/grated)	100 g	3½ oz
Vegan choc bits	155 g	5½ oz
Vegan margarine	225 g	8 oz

Oven Temperatures

Celsius	Fahrenheit	Gas mark
120	250	1
150	300	2
160	320	3
180	350	4
190	375	5
200	400	6
220	430	7
230	450	8
250	480	9

Liquid Measures

Cup	Metric	Imperial
¼ cup	63 ml	2¼ fl oz
½ cup	125 ml	4½ fl oz
¾ cup	188 ml	6⅔ fl oz
1 cup	250 ml	8¾ fl oz
1¾ cup	438 ml	15½ fl oz
2 cups	500 ml	17½ fl oz
4 cups	1 litre	35 fl oz

Spoon	Metric	Imperial
¼ teaspoon	1.25 ml	1/25 fl oz
½ teaspoon	2.5 ml	1/12 fl oz
1 teaspoon	5 ml	⅙ fl oz
1 tablespoon	15 ml	½ fl oz

Weight Measures

Metric	Imperial
10 g	¼ oz
15 g	½ oz
20 g	¾ oz
30 g	1 oz
60 g	2 oz
115 g	4 oz (¼ lb)
125 g	4½ oz
145 g	5 oz
170 g	6 oz
185 g	6½ oz
200 g	7 oz
225 g	8 oz (½ lb)
300 g	10½ oz
330 g	11½ oz
370 g	13 oz
400 g	14 oz
425 g	15 oz
455 g	16 oz (1 lb)
500 g	17½ oz (1 lb 1½ oz)
600 g	21 oz (1 lb 5 oz)
650 g	23 oz (1 lb 7 oz)
750 g	26½ oz (1 lb 10½ oz)
1000 g (1 kg)	35 oz (2 lb 3 oz)

INDEX